Mp3 Store and Clou

How to Store Your Music on the Cloud

By Amazon

Disclaimer

The information presented in this eBook is solely for educational purposes. While the author has made the utmost efforts to ensure accuracy of the contents herein, the readers are advised to follow the information at their own risk. This eBook does not consider personal situations, so it may not be suitable for every purpose.

All readers are encouraged to seek professional advice where needed. The author and/or publisher cannot be held responsible for any personal or commercial damage that results due to misinterpretation of guidelines and ideas presented in this eBook.

This eBook cannot be used as a substitute for professional advice.

Summary

While great things are expected of Amazon, Mp3 Store and Cloud Player are two of the most talked about topics these days. This is because Kindle, which was initially known for reading books and later, appeared as a smart device that connects you with the ever-expanding online world, was never seen as something that could be used for music.

Indeed, music and Kindle makes a very awkward, but very interesting combination. Kindle has now evolved more than ever, providing you space on the cloud for your music. Yes, that's correct! Now you can take music with you on the go as the cloud that carries all your favorite tracks will be following you wherever you go.

Ever thought you can have a transparent database for storing your favorite tracks and music? Well, Kindle has made this a reality by offering users a personalized space to store their favorite music on the cloud, which can be accessed anywhere and at any hour of the day.

This book has all the information you have been looking to make the most out of the Mp3 Store and Cloud player like a pro.

Keep reading till the end and enjoy!

Introduction to Amazon Cloud Player and MP3 Store

To put it simple, Amazon Cloud Player is an online storage service designed especially to secure your music on the cloud so that you can store and enjoy digital music on the go.

Together with the convenience of buying music directly from the Amazon MP3 store, it is also possible to upload any digital music of your collection that you have collected in different ways such as through recorded internet streams, audio ripped CDs, digital music services of download from legal and free sources, etc.

Once you successfully stored your music on the Amazon cloud, you can easily stream it using various smart devices, including tablets, Smartphones and even your computer at home.

No more living in the fair of losing your entire collection, especially if you are a music enthusiast. While a disc or a USB storage device can be stolen or lost, the main benefit and charm of storing your music on a digital, transparent platform is that you enjoy a disaster recovery option.

Welcome to the world of Amazon MP3 Store and Cloud Player and enjoy the accessibility and security of your music like never before.

The Musical Revolution – Music on the Cloud

If Amazon Cloud Player is a new concept for you, then simply understand that it is an online service that allows you to upload, store and stream music through various supported devices.

To begin this incredible experience of a lifetime, you are allowed to use 250 songs of storage for absolutely no cost. However, you can always extend the storage space by purchasing digital music through Amazon MP3 player. The good news is, the purchased storage will never override the free space available for you in the beginning.

In order to upload music on the Amazon Cloud Player, you need to have one thing – an Amazon Account. Once you loaded the songs to the cloud, you can access and listen to your favorite tracks (via streaming) on your computer through browser, android devices, Kindle Fire and even on your iPod and iPhone.

The step by step guide for you is covered later in the book.

Taking Music Wherever You Go – The Response and Acceptance

Since people are becoming increasingly tech savvy these days, it was easier for Amazon MP3 Store and Cloud Player to make a space in the crowd. People are very comfortable with the idea of storing and carrying their music on the cloud without the fear of losing it.

Thus, it can be said that the response and acceptance from the people received by Amazon Cloud Player and MP3 was incredible. It was even noticed that many Amazon accounts were only made for the sake of enjoying this amazing service offered by Amazon.

Your Storage Options

There are different storage options depending on whether you are using a premium service by paying subscription fee or using the free version of the Cloud Player.

As mentioned earlier, the free version of the player allows you to store up to 250 tracks of your choice without charging you any fee.

On the other hand, the premium version allows you to upload up to 250,000 songs and charges $24.99 per year for the service.

You can choose a storage option that fulfills your requirement.

Why Amazon MP3 Store Should Be Your First Choice?

Indeed, more information on Cloud Player and MP3 Store will excite you. Lately, Amazon MP3 Store is becoming the first choice for people to purchase music. Want to know why? Keep reading.

Join the Largest Online Playlist with More Than 20 Million Songs

The collection of music Amazon MP3 Store offers is beyond your imagination. It is loaded with 20 millions songs including a wide array of artists and all the bestselling albums you could think of.

The prices are reasonable too with full albums starting from $7.99. You can even purchase a single track which will cost you as low as $0.99.

The wide range of options allows you to shop according to your favorite tracks, music artists and albums from your Smartphone, Android tablet, Kindle Fire, iPod, iPad and iPhone. Purchasing from Amazon MP3 Store also enables you to directly transfer your tracks to the Cloud Player, which will automatically create a secure backup for your entire music collection.

Import Music from Any Supported Source to Amazon Cloud Player

As mentioned earlier, your tracks from the MP3 store will be automatically uploaded to the secure backup of Amazon Cloud player. However, it also introduces a feature called 'music importer' that allows you to import music to the cloud player from any supported source. Once the music is uploaded, it is available to be used in the Cloud Player anywhere you like.

Easy Access to Your Music Collection

One of the most important reasons people are storing their music on the cloud because of its easy access. Any piece of music uploaded on the Amazon Cloud Player can be downloaded and played anywhere you like on your Smartphones, Android tablets, iPod touch, iPhone, iPad as well as your Kindle Fire. Once the tracks are downloaded, you do not require an internet connection to play them.

Buying Amazon Music from MP3 Store

New Albums

Page 1 of 7

Blurred Lines
Robin Thicke
(2)
$8.99

The Wrong Side Of Heaven And The...
› Five Finger Death Punch
(17)
$8.99

All People
› Michael Franti & Spearhead
(6)
$6.99

New Songs

Page 1 of 7

Everything Has Changed
Taylor Swift

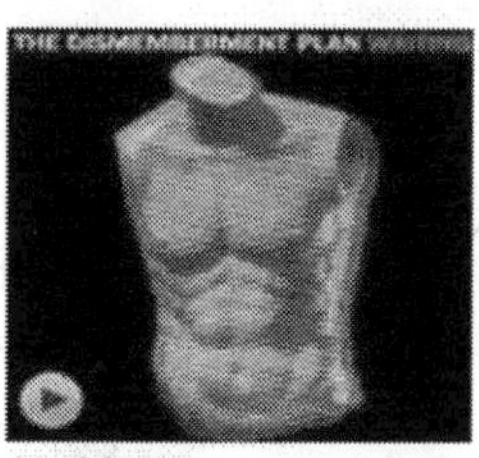

Waiting
The Dismemberment Plan

A.M.
Chris Young

Top Albums $6.99 or Less

Night Visions (Deluxe)
› Imagine Dragons
(723)
$5.99

Unorthodox Jukebox [Explicit]
› Bruno Mars
(726)

Save Rock And Roll
› Fall Out Boy
(205)
$5.99

You can only purchase a track from the Amazon MP3 store if you have an Amazon account, a 1- Click payment method by a United States Bank and a United States billing address.

Visit www.Amazon.com and set up your account now, in case you already don't have one. Instructions for you to follow will appear on the screen. Once the account has been created, check out the music collection at the Amazon MP3 store. Search for your favorite music to buy it.

Step 1 – Amazon MP3 can easily be accessed from your web browser on your desktop, Kindle tablets, android tablets and phones and other Smartphones. Click or tap on the title of the track to check the details of the tracks that interest you.

Step 2 – On the detail page, click on Buy mp3 album/song with 1-Click and proceed.

Load your Apple Gadgets with Amazon MP3 Store Collection

Got those amazing Apple gadgets? Now you can shop at Amazon MP3 Store and buy your favorite tracks and albums using the Cloud Player application for iOS.

This easy-to-use app allows you to explore Amazon MP3 Store for your favorite music that you can purchase for your Apple devices including iPod, iPad and/or iPhone.

Unfortunately, there is one limitation of these great applications. They only allow USA customers to purchase music from the store for iPod and iPhone.

Step 1 – Look for tracks or music albums you wish to purchase and confirm your order by tapping the **BUY** option. You will be charged against your purchase using your 1-Click payment method and the track or album will be automatically loaded to your Cloud Player.

Your Amazon MP3 as a Giveaway

Ever gifted music before? While many people have exchanged Cassettes and CDs as gifts previously, sharing music on the cloud is the latest trend in the market. Purchase an mp3 and gift it to your friends and family.

The person who receives music as a gift can download or play music using the Cloud Player or can even exchange the track or album for an Amazon.com Gift Card.

Step 1 – In order to purchase a track for friends or family members, access the Amazon MP3 Store through your Amazon account.

Step 2 – Search for the track you want to gift to someone and then click or tap on **GIVE AS A GIFT** button present right under the **BUY** button to proceed.

Step 3 – You will be asked to specify an email address of the recipient. Continue to confirm the order and sent the track to the person's email address.

If you have received music as a gift, go to your inbox and click **GET YOUR GIFT NOW.** Follow the instructions to claim your gift on Amazon.com. Next, click on **DOWNLOAD YOUR MP3 GIFT** and continue after submitting your account details.

You can download the music or play music directly in the Cloud Player and enjoy.

Taking Music Higher – Importing Your Tracks to the Cloud

So you have your music collection on your computer, Windows Media Player or iTunes?

If yes, the good news for you is that your favorite music can now be transferred to your

Amazon Cloud Player. **The Imported** can be used to successfully transfer your collection to the secured backup of the cloud. However, make sure you have the latest Adobe Flash installed on your device and the software is enabled.

Step 1 – To install Amazon Music Importer, first visit Amazon Cloud Player for Web through your browser. Any popular browsers such as Safari, Firefox and Internet Explorer can be used to proceed.

Step 2 – Click on the **IMPORT YOUR MUSIC** option followed by **DOWNLOAD NOW** to continue. The installation will automatically begin. Make sure you follow all the instructions that you come across on the screen.

Add Tracks to the Amazon Cloud Player

Once you have the importer on your computer, the software will look for permission to search your music libraries automatically. While doing so will help you upload your entire music collection in one go, you can choose to do it manually to upload only selected music in your folders. While this is time consuming, you will have a more personalized playlist on the Cloud Player.

If you chose to automatically let the software scan your music folders, all the tracks in Windows Media Player, iTunes and other relevant folders will pop up in your Amazon Music Importer. Click **IMPORT ALL** and transfer all your music data.

Cloud Player and Supported File Formats

File formats can create a lot of trouble for you if they are not supported while importing or uploading music on the Cloud Player. The following file formats are recommended:

- mp3
- ogg (Ogg Vorbis audio files)
- flac (Free Lossless Audio Codec files)
- m4a and AAC files for Windows and Mac including purchases from iTunes store.
- aiff (Audio Interchange Audio Format)
- wav
- wma (Windows Media Audio files)

Streaming Music from Far Above

Stream music from the cloud and listen to your favorite tracks in the one and only Amazon Cloud. You can listen to the tracks saved on the Cloud Player using the Amazon MP3 app, Amazon Cloud Player app or simply by using Cloud Player for web on your computer. Music stored on the Cloud Player can be streamed on all compatible devices.

To do so:

Step 1 – Access Amazon Cloud Player on your any compatible device. Explore your collection and select a music piece and click/tap on **PLAY.** The track will instantly begin playing provided you are connected to a good internet connection.

Step 2 – Check for your internet access point or wireless signals in case you are unable to load the track immediately. Sometimes music can take time to play, be patient.

Step 3 – Downloaded music can be played even without an internet connection.

Creating a Personalized Playlist in the Cloud Player

It is easy to make a playlist in Amazon Cloud Player. Open your tracks and click on the check boxes placed right next to the tracks that you wish to add in your new playlist. Once all the tracks are selected, click **ADD TO PLAYLIST.** Check out the example below to see how you do it.

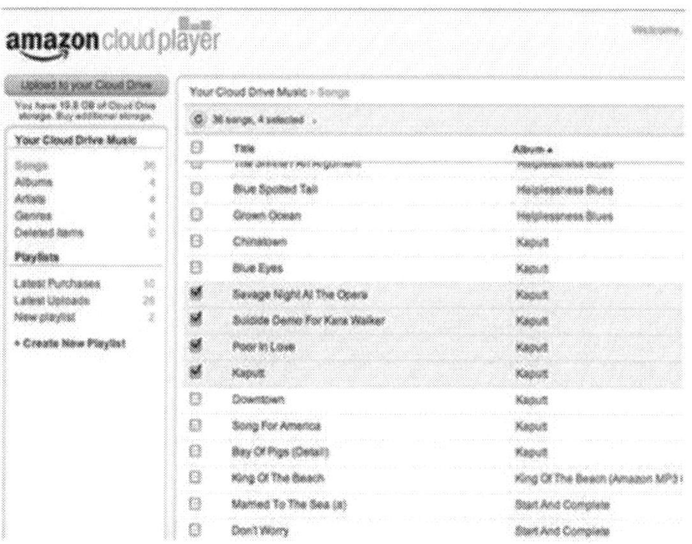

You can also make edits and delete tracks using a similar method. Select the check boxes of tracks you wish to delete and then click **DELETE** to continue. The deleted tracks are sent to the **Deleted Items** and can be restored. However, if you permanently wish to delete these tracks, go to the **DELETED ITEMS** and click **EMPTY ALL DELETED ITEMS.**

Cloud and Your Computer – The Musical Connection

Technology has lately established a musical connection between your computer and the Cloud in the shape of Amazon Cloud Player. Now you can store your music collection on the cloud from any compatible device where you have stored all your music and can enjoy music from the cloud on your computer by downloading or streaming tracks.

No more transferring music from your devices and gadgets to your computer because a single platform can be accessed from various platforms to get all the tracks you have stored on the cloud. Read on to learn how.

Enjoy Music from the Cloud to Your Desktop Using MP3 Downloader

There is a feature of Amazon Cloud Player called Amazon MP3 Downloader. This is supported by both Macintosh and Windows PCs and you can use it with your web browser to enhance y our downloading experience and make it more interesting.

As far as Windows PC is concerned, the software is only compatible with Windows Vista, Windows XP and Windows 7. On the other hand, if you have a Mac computer, then make sure you are running on Mac OS X 10.4 on Intel-Based Hardware. In addition, you will also need an Adobe AIR version 3.3.x.

Amazon MP3 Downloader is an incredible software that enables you to download tracks from the Cloud Player to your computer and sent it to Windows Media Player or iTunes. To do so, first of all log in to your Amazon account and then install the downloader from the following link:

http://www.amazon.com/gp/dmusic/help/amd.html/.

Install the Amazon MP3 Downloader

We recommend installing the Amazon MP3 Downloader before your first purchase. It is required for multiple-song downloads and makes downloading songs fast and easy.

Click **Install** to install the Amazon MP3 Downloader and save all eligible past and future Amazon music purchases and matched music to Cloud Player.

☐ I have read and accept the Terms of Use.

Install — For Windows XP, Windows Vista, and Windows 7. Download takes less than 90 seconds.

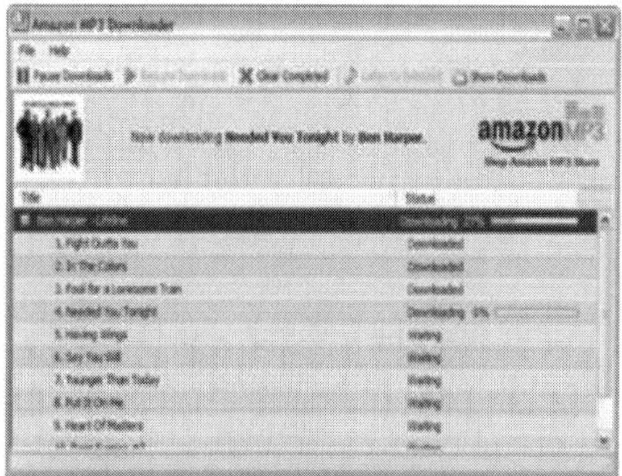

Click on the **Install** button, as can be seen on the illustration above, and follow the instructions to download the software successfully. The operating system will be automatically detected to download the compatible version of the software.

Step By Step Guide to Downloading Music to Your Computer

Once the Amazon MP3 Downloader is successfully installed on your computer, you can enjoy your entire music collection from the Amazon Cloud Player right on your personal computer.

Step 1 – While you can directly listen to the songs by accessing the Cloud Player online, you must log in to your Amazon Cloud Player account and mark the check boxes for the tracks you wish to download.

Step 2 – Next, click on the **DOWNLOAD** button to download the selected tracks and your music will automatically be loaded to your iTunes, Windows Media Player or desktop (as per your selection).

It is important to note here that in case you have not downloaded and installed the downloader software, you will be prompted when you will try to download the track from the Cloud Player. However, downloading a single song does not require software. Skip the installation and download the track easily using your computer's browser.

Searching for Downloaded

After downloading the file, usually people face difficulty in finding it. While you can specify where you would like to save your file when downloading on the computer, tracks or albums downloaded from Amazon Cloud Player are directly saved to the app on your device's Cloud Player application.

Also, check for the downloaded file in the default download folder on your computer or device to find the tracks you have downloaded.

There is also a **DOWNLOAD FOLDER** in the Amazon MP3 Downloader. In case you fail to find the track, launch the Amazon MP3 downloader and view the download folder. Your track is also saved on **MY MUSIC** default folder on your computer.

There are various ways of finding the downloaded track. Choose whichever you find more comfortable.

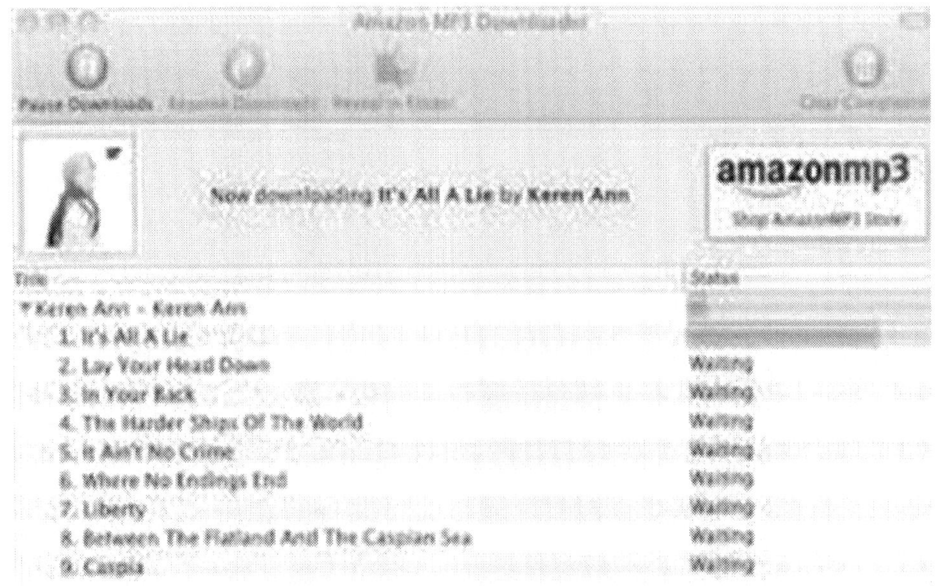

Tracks on Your Computer

AMZ Files and Your Collection

While purchasing music from the MP3 Store using your PCs web browser, you will be prompted with a dialogue box asking you to save or open a .amz file. This message will only appear once you have Amazon MP3 Downloader installed on your PC.

If you are purchasing a track using the Amazon MP3 Store on web, always select **OPEN** whenever prompted. By doing so, the Amazon MP3 Downloader will be automatically launched and will download the track to your PC without any hassle.

Kindle Devices – The Most Compatible Ones for Buying and Enjoying your Music

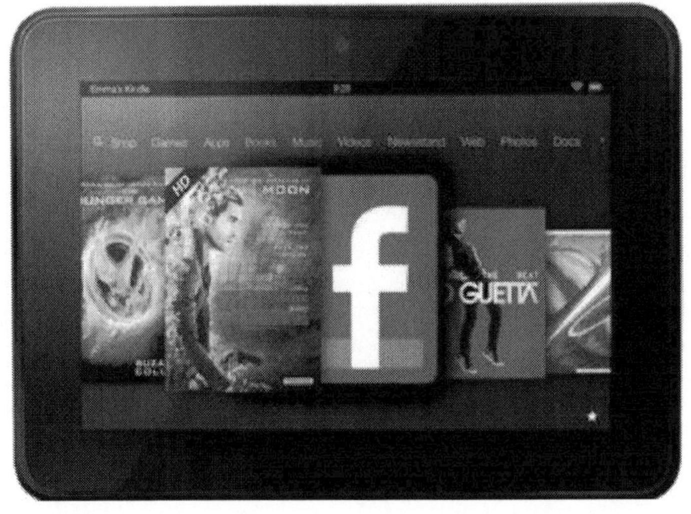

The Supportive Kindle Devices

Accessing and buying from Amazon MP3 Store and using Amazon Cloud Player on Kindle Device does not require any additional procedures or processes. Enjoy music on a device which was initially popular for reading eBooks only. However, with technology, Kindle devices have evolved rapidly, now bringing music to you wherever you are all the way from the cloud.

To enjoy music using your Cloud Player on your Kindle device, go to the **MUSIC** option and select **STORE.**

Doing so will directly take you to the Amazon MP3 Store where you can make the most out of the incredible MP3 deals and promotions.

The plethora of music options are waiting for you under Amazon MP3 Store, where you can easily browse to get your favorite music available under different categories including New Releases, Bestsellers, Genres, etc.

Purchasing the Tracks

Getting your favorite tracks from MP3 Store for your amazing Kindle device is just the same as for any other compatible device. Just know what you want and explore the never-ending music options at the Amazon MP3 Store. If you have an album or track in your mind, just enter it in the search bar and proceed to see the results. The results will show all the relevant tracks or albums in a list.

Tap the **BUY** or **GET** option to proceed with your purchase. The payment method you have prescribed will be processed and you will become the owner of the track. Your music will be automatically uploaded on your Cloud Player on your Kindle device.

To do so, access your library by tapping on **GO TO YOUR LIBRARY** option. Here you can see the list of tracks purchased. Download any track you like on your Kindle.

To buy more, tap **CONTINUE SHOPPING** and you will be taken back to the MP3 Store to buy more amazing music.

Operating Cloud Player on Your Kindle

You have a Cloud Library in your Kindle, where you will have all the tracks you have downloaded from the Cloud Player. To go to the library, tap **MUSIC** on the Home Screen and select **CLOUD.** In addition to the music from the Cloud Player, you will also find iTunes and music imported from your computer here. Tap on any track to play and enjoy the music.

It is important to remember that Cloud Player will only work if your device is connected to the internet. Also, you need to have a good internet connection to listen to music smoothly. Cloud Player is online music storage, thus you need to be online on your Kindle device in order to view the library and play songs online.

The only way you can listen to Cloud Player tracks without the internet is by downloading the tracks to your Kindle tablet.

Reviewing Amazon MP3 Store in Detail

Why is Amazon MP3 Store enjoying such hype? Because the offerings of Amazon MP3 Store have become an open threat to iTunes Store!

With its wide array of digital music store, Amazon MP3 Store has raised the bar for paid-for music services online by offering customers by providing DRM-free Content. Here is a detailed review of Amazon MP3 Store, which will greatly justify why it has become one of the most popular online music galleries to date. Keep reading.

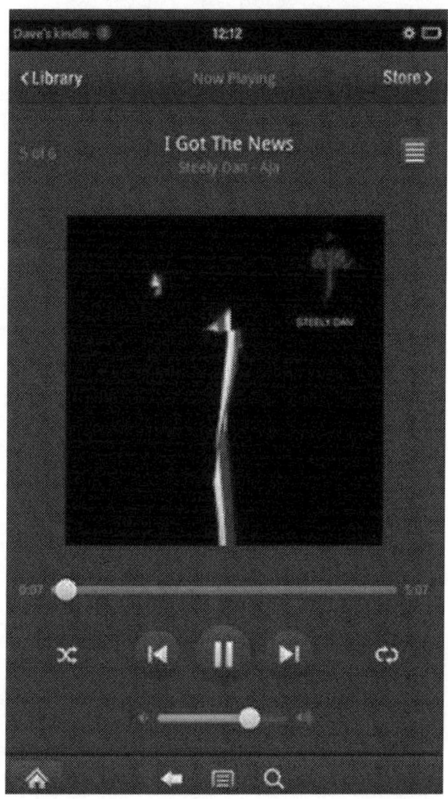

Discussing Pros and Cons

PROS:

- The tracks you will find here are DRM-free MP3s.
- Offers more than 20 million tracks.
- Offers great value for money.

CONS:

- The service is limited to people residing in USA only.
- Amazon MP3 downloader software is used only when multiple songs are purchased.

Service Features

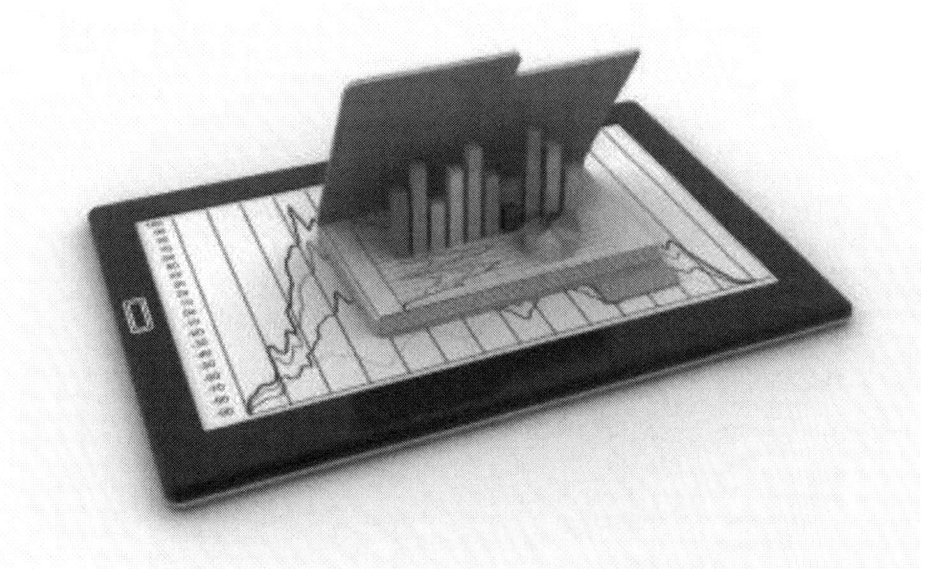

Pricing Structure

The price for a single track you find at Amazon MP3 Store falls between $0.89 and $0.99.

The price for albums falls between $4.99 and $9.00+.

Digital Delivery of Music

Amazon MP3 follows a very simple and easy to understand system that enables you to choose the tracks you want and simply download them. It is just like downloading from iTunes Store. Amazon customers do not need to subscribe for the services again. You can get started by simply logging in to your Amazon account.

Previewing the List of Albums and Songs

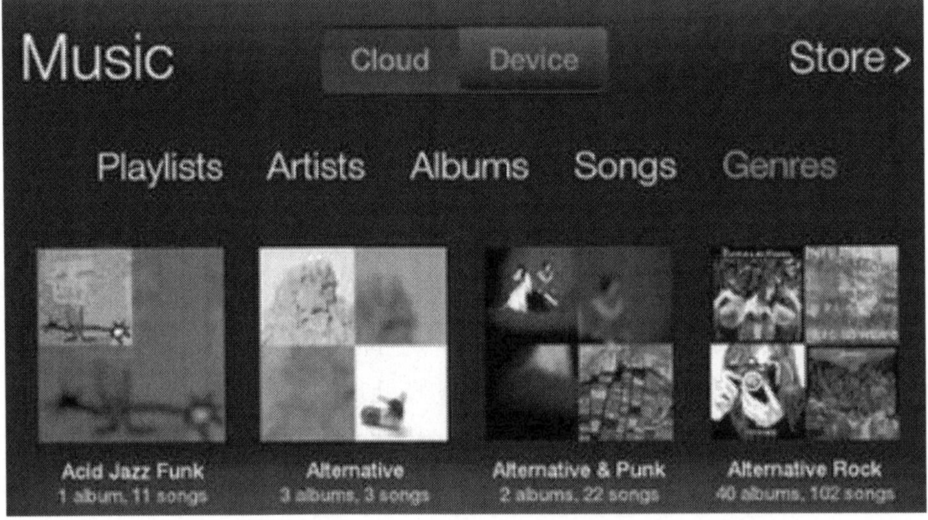

Before buying an album or a single track, you can listen to a 30-sec clip of the song through an embedded player to help you confirm whether it is the same song or album you have been looking for. There are various useful functions in the player such as pause/play buttons, next/previous track button, and volume control.

There is more very important feature of Amazon's embedded music player. It is the **PREVIEW ALL** button that allows you to listen to multiple songs or the entire album's short clips in a single go.

Website Content

The choice of 20 million songs offered by Amazon MP3 Store is extremely respectable. There is indeed a long list of different genres of music that are officially published as a homepage on their website.

As an alternative, you can find the song, artist and albums to download from the MP3 Store by simply putting it up in the search box. Select a particular genre of the song to narrow down your results to getting more accurate ones.

The Purchasing Process

Just like other stores operated on Amazon.com, the system and interface of buying music from Amazon MP3 Store is quite similar. Although the layout and design can create confusion at times, all you need to focus on is the **BUY** button in orange, conveniently placed next to the album or track. This makes the overall procedure quite simple and straightforward.

The good news is that Amazon MP3 Store also uses the 1-Click buy option that allows you to automatically utilize your card details to credit your account by purchasing the track or the album instantly.

Software

Introduction to Amazon MP3 Downloader

Amazon MP3 Downloader is download manager software that allows you to download multiple files at one time much easily. Once the software is installed, it will automatically run every time you purchase tracks from the Amazon MP3 Store. However, the only pitfall to this software is that if you wish to buy an album, then you are required to install it in order to finish the transaction completely.

This could be annoying for some customers who are not comfortable in downloading multiple software on their computer for the sake of securing their music.

Technical Details

Audio Formats:

- Compression – VBR
- Audio bitstream rate – 256 kbps
- MPEG – 1 Audio Layer 3 (MP3)

Download Software for Amazon MP3:

Available for the platforms mentioned below:

- Linux – Debian 4 Etch, Open SUSE 10.3, Fedora 8, and Ubuntu 7.10 Gutsy.
- Mac OS X 10.4 or higher.
- Windows Vista or XP.

Bottom Line

When it comes to services, indeed Amazon has raised the bar and has been delivering excellent services that are not only useful but user friendly. Also, it provides downloads that are absolutely compatible because of the unprotected MP3 formats.

As far as the prices are concerned, it is believed that they are keen offering single tracks for as low as 99 cents and a few albums rated for less than $4.99. This makes the overall service offered by Amazon excellent value for money.

The wide range of music, artists, genre, and type of media are added benefits that you can make the most of using this incredible music service. While there are some shortcomings in all the systems, Amazon provides powerful digital music service that can give any established digital services a serious run for the money.

Enjoy Cloud Player at Last!

Your ultimate solution for storing your entire music collection has been introduced by Amazon. Amazon MP3 Store and Cloud Player are the two resources that you need in order to store your current music collection and update it with the best of the best tracks in future. In short, Amazon MP3 Store and Cloud Player make the perfect combination for all music enthusiasts who just cannot live without their music.

For a passionate music lover, nothing could be better than having a personalized storage on the cloud in the form of cloud player and a music store with more than 20 million tracks. An Amazon account is all that you need in order to make the most out of these two incredible services offered by Amazon.

Your music will remain on the go with you, regardless of where you are. Whenever you like, just pull out your smart device and enjoy your own selected list of tracks. So not only this feature allows you to secure a safe backup for your music collection, keeping your music on the cloud also helps you to access it whenever and wherever you like.

All crucial aspects of Amazon MP3 Store and Cloud Player are covered in detail in this book. The step by step instructions can be easily followed to avoid any hassle in experiencing your own world of music, which can be accessed on your own smart device, whenever you like.

No one can stop you from keeping yourself connected with your music if you have the Cloud Player on your Kindle and all the other supported devices such as tablets, iPods, iPads, iPhone, computer and other Smartphones.

While keeping 250 songs in your Cloud Player is absolutely free of cost, you can store up to 250,000 songs on a safe backup platform by paying a very reasonable price per year to keep up with your Amazon Cloud Experience. Take your musical experience beyond skies all the way up to the clouds where there is no risk of losing them or any theft. Your music collection will remain how you like it till the end.

Indeed, there is no limit to music or the passion for it. So if you share the same passion, let Amazon MP3 Store and Cloud Player help you keep up with it!

Printed in Great Britain
by Amazon